Rise Above The Competition:

Mastering Business Pursuit and Career Growth

Leah Gordon

TABLE OF CONTENT

INTRODUCTION

In a world overflowing with desire and contest, this book arises as a reference point of direction and motivation. Inside its pages, perusers are welcomed on an enlightening excursion towards proficient greatness and individual satisfaction. Yet, what separates this book from the heap of self improvement guides flooding the market? It's the commitment of strengthening, the affirmation that with the right instruments and attitude, anybody can climb higher than ever of achievement. Envision a scene where difficulties are open doors, where misfortunes are just venturing stones, and where every deterrent is an opportunity to hit one out of the ballpark more brilliant. Through canny systems, noteworthy counsel, and convincing accounts, this book furnishes perusers with the abilities and certainty to explore the consistently developing territory of business and vocation development. Whether you're a carefully prepared business visionary or a sprouting proficient, "Rise above the competition: Mastering Business Pursuit and Career Growth" is your guide to overcoming the cutthroat scene and arising triumphant in your quest for progress.

CHAPTER 1

Don't Pursue Your Passion

In a world where passion is often touted as the key to success, it may seem counterintuitive to suggest otherwise. After all, the idea of following our passions resonates deeply with our desire for fulfillment and purpose. However, the reality is that blindly pursuing our passions can sometimes lead to disappointment and disillusionment. While passion is undoubtedly a driving force behind success, it is not always enough to sustain a fulfilling career.

One of the disadvantages of relying only on passion is the restricted focus it results in. When we become fixated on a single love, we may unintentionally limit our prospects and neglect other areas where we could excel. This tunnel vision can keep us from pursuing new interests and finding unexpected avenues to achievement.

Furthermore, passion solely does not ensure competency or skill in a specific profession. Success frequently necessitates a combination of enthusiasm, ability, and knowledge. Simply being enthusiastic about something does not inevitably qualify us to excel at it. Education, training, and experience are vital for developing the required skills and knowledge.

Consider the case of Steve Jobs, the co-founder of Apple Inc. While Jobs is sometimes lauded for his enthusiasm and vision, his rise to prominence was not primarily motivated by emotion. Jobs first became interested in calligraphy and Eastern mysticism before discovering prospects in computing and design. His love for exquisite design and user-friendly technology eventually led to the development of devices that transformed the technology sector. Jobs admitted, "You have to find what you love... The only way to perform an excellent job is to like what you do." Still, his brilliance came from the marriage of emotion, imagination, and technical know-how.

Similarly, Oprah Winfrey's career was built on a series of serendipitous opportunities rather than a single passion-driven goal. Winfrey began as a news anchor before transitioning to hosting a daytime talk show, where she discovered her aptitude for storytelling and connecting with people. Her ability to adapt and seize chances helped her become one of today's most important media leaders.

The experiences of Jobs, Winfrey, and numerous other brilliant people serve as a reminder that enthusiasm alone is insufficient to ensure success. While passion can fuel our motivation and objectives, it is our willingness to explore new pathways, enhance our talents, and seize opportunities that ultimately defines our path.

To summarize, while passion is absolutely vital, it should not be the main determining factor in shaping our careers. By keeping open to new chances, cultivating diverse skills, and embracing lifelong learning, we can forge routes to success that go beyond our hobbies. We will address these in the subsequent chapters of this book.

CHAPTER 2

The Precision Of Workmanship

In today's competitive landscape, the ability to deliver quality work with precision and skill is more critical than ever. Whether you're pursuing a career in business, technology, or any other field, honing your skills can give you a significant edge over the competition. While passion may provide the initial drive, it is the precision of your workmanship that ultimately sets you apart and propels you to success.

One of the primary advantages of honing your craftsmanship is the ability to consistently create products that exceed expectations. Precision requires attention to detail, accuracy, and a dedication to perfection in every activity you perform. By mastering your craft and consistently producing high-quality work, you build a reputation for reliability and professionalism that earns the trust and respect of colleagues, clients, and employers alike.

Take the example of Elon Musk, the CEO of SpaceX and Tesla Inc. Musk is well-known for his ambitious vision and unwavering determination, as well as his rigorous attention to detail and emphasis on precision in all aspects of his work. From creating cutting-edge spaceships to changing the electric vehicle business,

Musk's dedication to quality has been a driving force in his success.

Similarly, another leader that recognizes the value of accuracy in craftsmanship is Jeff Bezos, the creator and former CEO of Amazon. Bezos is credited with establishing the "two-pizza rule," which states that in order to maximize productivity and reduce red tape, teams should be small enough to feed two pizzas. Amazon's success has been largely attributed to its focus on streamlining operations and getting rid of waste, which has enabled the business to provide outstanding value to customers all over the world.

Developing accuracy in your work not only improves your reputation professionally but also increases your sense of fulfillment and personal satisfaction. There is a sense of pride and success that comes from striving for perfection in all that you do, even if you don't get paid for it. Furthermore, becoming an expert in your field creates new avenues for development and progress, enabling you to take your profession to new heights.

In the end, your level of precision in your job speaks volumes about your discipline, commitment to perfection, and dedication. By consistently improving your abilities, accepting new challenges, and aiming for excellence in all that you do, you establish yourself as a unique performer in your industry and provide the groundwork for long-term prosperity and contentment. In conclusion, your success is ultimately determined by the accuracy of your work, even though emotion may spur your desire and ambition. You can stand out in a competitive field and accomplish your professional objectives by concentrating on honing your trade, producing outstanding work, and never giving up on greatness.

CHAPTER 3

Avoid The Control Trap

Giving over control of your career to others is a common mistake in the fast-paced, cutthroat business world of today. Taking charge of your professional future can often be overshadowed by the temptation of security and a consistent paycheck, regardless of the size of your employer. However, long-term success and fulfillment require actively creating your own career path and avoiding the control trap. Being able to take the initiative and set your own goals is one of the biggest benefits of being your own boss, even in a regular work environment. While it is essential to respect authority and follow company protocols, there's also ample opportunity to carve out your niche, showcase your unique skills and talents, and distinguish yourself from your peers. By proactively seeking out new challenges, taking on additional responsibilities, and demonstrating leadership potential, you position yourself as a valuable asset to your organization and increase your visibility and influence within the company.

Take, for example, Sheryl Sandberg, Facebook's COO. Despite her high-ranking position at one of the world's most powerful corporations, Sandberg has always retained a sense of independence and control over her career path. Throughout her time at Facebook, she has been an outspoken supporter of women in leadership positions, led efforts to promote diversity and inclusion, and used her influence to impact positive change both within the company and in the broader tech industry. Sandberg has established herself as a respected leader and role model for ambitious professionals throughout the world by being true to her ideals and actively influencing her own career trajectory.

Author, businessman, and investor Tim Ferriss is another person who has successfully escaped the control trap and paved his own route to success. Early in his career, Ferriss had many obstacles and disappointments, but he refused to accept mediocrity and instead concentrated on creating his own name and brand. Ferriss' bestselling books, famous podcast, and innovative business endeavors have inspired millions of people to take control of their lives, pursue their passions, and reach their full potential.

Avoiding the control trap not only improves your career possibilities but also creates fresh avenues for personal development and fulfillment. You can give your work meaning and purpose and establish the groundwork for long-term success and fulfillment by actively searching out experiences that fit with your values and taking charge of your career.

In conclusion, being your own boss and eschewing the control trap are critical for career success and fulfillment—even in traditional employment structures. You can stand out from the crowd, have a greater impact, and accomplish your job objectives by demonstrating your special abilities and talents, taking the initiative, and actively creating your own career path.

CHAPTER 4

Learn To Hear, And Hear To Understand

"Education is the ability to listen to almost anything without losing your temper or your self-confidence."

-Robert Frost

The capacity to listen and fully comprehend in a world full with noise and distractions is a rare and useful quality. This chapter delves into the significance of possessing teachable, perceptive, and cautious qualities in your quest of business and professional development. A key component of success is having an open mind and being eager to take in fresh insights and knowledge from others. Being receptive to criticism and direction is crucial for ongoing development and progress, regardless of your experience level or career stage. This applies to both new graduates and seasoned professionals seeking to progress in their careers. Through proactively pursuing chances to acquire knowledge from mentors, peers, and professionals in the field, you may enhance your expertise, hone your abilities, and maintain a competitive advantage in a constantly changing business environment.

Furthermore, effective communication and the development of relationships depend on the capacity for sympathetic and attentive listening. Understanding the wants and concerns of others is crucial for developing collaboration, establishing trust, and reaching win-win results whether you're leading a team, working on a project together, or negotiating a sale. You may fortify your professional bonds and improve your efficacy as a leader and team member by taking the time to listen intently to the viewpoints of others and to demonstrate real interest and empathy.

In addition, success in company and career advancement demands not only a teachable quality but also a sharp observational and cautious sense. In today's fast-paced and dynamic business environment, being able to anticipate trends, identify opportunities, and adapt to changing circumstances is essential for staying ahead of the competition and achieving your goals. By cultivating a habit of mindfulness and awareness, you can develop a strategic mindset and make informed decisions that lead to success and prosperity.

Consider the investing success of Warren Buffett. Known for his legendary ability to spot undervalued assets and invest wisely, Buffett attributes much of his success to his insatiable curiosity and relentless pursuit of knowledge. By constantly learning and observing the world around him, Buffett has been able to identify lucrative investment opportunities and build a vast fortune over the course of his career.

In conclusion, you may position yourself for success and accomplish your professional goals by encouraging a lifelong learning mentality, actively listening to others, and remaining aware of the world around you.

CHAPTER 5

Be Bold In Your Thinking And Actions

Recognize that courage and assertiveness have the transformational potential to propel professional and business success. As the adage goes, "Fortune favors the bold". The capacity for audacious thought and decisive action might be the difference between realizing your full potential and accomplishing your objectives in a world of intense competition and abundant opportunities.

The courage to take chances and explore unfamiliar ground is the foundation of daring thought and action. Being willing to take risks and embrace uncertainty is crucial for growth and advancement, whether you're starting a new business, making a pitch for a creative idea, or seeking a job opportunity. You can overcome challenges and achieve extraordinary success by accepting the uncertainty and grasping chances with conviction and confidence.

Furthermore, being strong includes something other than taking risks; it additionally includes having the guts to shield your standards and convictions notwithstanding criticism or misfortune. Being courageous in your beliefs can motivate people and bring about significant change, whether you're supporting something you have confidence in, restricting the current quo, or talking truth to drive. Your organization, your neighborhood, and the world at large can all benefit from your voice and stand on topics that are important to you.

Consider the innovative entrepreneur Elon Musk. He is renowned for his daring objectives and forward-thinking vision, and he has transformed a variety of industries, including electric automobiles and space research. Musk has accomplished extraordinary success by having the guts to dream large and pursuing lofty objectives with unflinching resolve. His example has encouraged millions of people to imagine big and take risks in order to follow their own aspirations.

Bold ideas and deeds might not only help you succeed personally but also provide you an advantage in a competitive market. Being willing to take estimated risks and push the envelope of what's doable can assist you with standing apart from the opposition and set up a good foundation for yourself as a pioneer and trend-setter in your industry in today's fiercely competitive business world. Being brave in your approach can assist you with acquiring piece of the pie, draw clients, spike development, and lay out another plan of action — whether you're presenting another item, breaking into another industry, or fostering a pristine business system.

In summary, by accepting risk, standing up for your convictions, and pushing the limits of what's possible, you may achieve remarkable results and leave a lasting impression on the world around you. Dare to dream big, take bold steps, and seize the chances that await!

9 798880 409860